Handy Arkansas Genealogy Handbook

I0450175

By Gary L. Morris

©2015 Gary L. Morris

ISBN-13: 978-1507660980

ISBN-10: 1507660987

Table of Contents

Notes

Genealogical Research in Arkansas

Tracing ancestry in the state of Arkansas faces its own set of challenges as well as many unique rewards. There are many historical and genealogical records available for the state, and we know just where to find them. To get you started in tracing your ancestry, on this page we will introduce you to those records, and help you to understand:

1. What they are
2. Where to find them
3. How to use them

These records can be found both online and off, so we'll introduce you to online websites, indexes and databases, as well as brick-and-mortar repositories and other institutions that will help with your research in Arkansas. So that you will have a more comprehensive understanding of these records, we have provided a brief history of the "The Natural State" to illustrate what type of records may have been generated during specific time periods. That information will assist you in pinpointing times and locations on which to focus the search for your Arkansas ancestors.

A Brief History of Arkansas

Archaeologists have uncovered pottery and stone artefacts in the bluffs and mounds of Arkansas which show that people have inhabited the area for thousands of years. The Native Americans who originally inhabited Arkansas were the Choctaw, Cherokee, Caddos, Osage, Quapaws, and the very early Mound Builders and Bluff Dwellers.

Hernando de Soto was the first of the Europeans to enter the area, he arrived in 1541 looking fior gold which he never found. Two Frenchmen named Joliet and Marquette visited Arkansas briefly in 1673, and LaSalle claimed the region for France in 1682. De Tonti, known as the "Father of Arkansas" established the first European settlement in what was named Arkansas Post in 1686.

In 1803 Arkansas was acquired by the United States in the Louisiana purchase, and organized into a territory in 1819. Later, in 1821, the territorial capital was moved from Arkansas Post to Little Rock. There were over 60,000 residents of Arkansas by 1836, and it was declared the 25th state in that year.

In May 1861 Arkansas left the Union and entered the civil War. After the end of the Civil War in 1865, the Reconstruction era began, and dramatic changes occurred in the South. The Democrats regained power in 1874, and the present-day US Constitution was adopted in that same year. As early as 1875, Arkansas was known as the "Land of Opportunity" when a campaign was launched outside the state to attract new residents to the region. By 1900, the population had risen to 1.3 million.

In 1921, the first auto, gas, and oil taxes were levied to finance construction of paved roads and highways into Arkansas. The oil and natural gas reserves were discovered in the state which provided cheap and plentiful energy for many years. The increased use of farm machinery led to the consolidation of many small family-run farms into large farming corporations. Arkansans discovered in 1904 that rice could be grown there successfully, and it is now one of the state's most profitable crops. Arkansas has grown from vast wilderness to a thriving state with a population of 2.5 million. Advancements in lumbering, manufacturing, farming, tourism, and government have resulted in Arkansas being well-placed in the international market.

Important Genealogical Dates in Arkansas History

1700 - Area under French Civil Law

1763 – Ceded from France to Spain

1800 – Ceded from Spain to France

1803 – Part of the Louisiana Purchase

1805 – Part of Louisiana Territory

1812 – Part of Missouri territory

!819 – Organized as an individual Territory

1836 – Statehood

1862 – Cedes from the Union

1868 – Readmitted to Union

1874 – Adopts modern day Constitution.

Famous Battles Fought in Arkansas

Arkansas has a rich military past from its territorial period to the present. The information contained in accounts and other documentation of famous battles can be very effective in uncovering the military records of your ancestor. They can tell you what regiments fought in which battles, and often include the names and ranks of many officers and enlisted men. Following are some of the most famous battles fought in Arkansas and links to useful information about them.

The Battle of Arkansas Post (aka Battle of Fort Hindman) 1863 – Civil War

The Battle of Arkansas Post:
http://www.encyclopediaofarkansas.net/encyclopedia/entry-detail.aspx?entryID=525

Battle of Pea Ridge: http://www.civilwar.org/battlefields/pea-ridge.html

Battle of Prairie Grove 1862 (Civil War)

Battle of Prairie Grove:
http://www.encyclopediaofarkansas.net/encyclopedia/entry-detail.aspx?entryID=513

Common Arkansas Genealogical Issues and Resources to Overcome Them

Boundary Changes: A common obstacle when researching Arkansas ancestors are historical boundary changes. You could be searching for an ancestor's record in one county when in fact it is stored in a different one due to historical county boundary changes. The **Atlas of Historical County Boundaries** can help you to overcome that problem. It provides a chronological listing of every boundary change that has occurred in the history of Arkansas.

Atlas of Historical County Boundaries:
http://publications.newberry.org/ahcbp/documents/AR_Consolidated
_Chronology.htm#Consolidated_Chronology

Name Changes: Surname changes, variations, and misspellings can complicate genealogical research. It is important to check all spelling variations. Soundex, a program that indexes names by sound, is a useful first step, but you can't rely on it completely as some name variations result in different Soundex codes. The surnames could be different, but the first name may be different too. You can also find records filed under initials, middle names, and nicknames as well, so you will need to **get creative with surname variations** and spellings in order to cover all the possibilities. For help with surname variations read our instructional article on **How to Use Soundex**.

get creative with surname variations:
http://obituarieshelp.org/blog/?p=634

How to Use Soundex: http://obituarieshelp.org/blog/?p=505

Arkansas Genealogical Organizations and Archives

Genealogical resources include not only records, but the organizations that house them, or can direct you to them. These institutions include: *Archives, Libraries, Genealogical Societies, Family History Centers, Universities, Churches, and Museums.*

Following are links to their websites, their physical addresses, and a summary of the records you can find there.

Archives

Arkansas History Commission and Archives - an excellent array of genealogy records including: census records, county records, State government records, military records, Church and cemetery records, manuscripts, newspapers, photographs, maps, historical books and pamphlets, and more.

Arkansas History Commission and Archives
1 Capitol Mall
Little Rock, Arkansas 72201
Tel: (501) 682-6900

Arkansas History Commission and Archives: http://www.ark-ives.com/

Arkansas State Library - online databases such as the Biography and Genealogy Master Index, and the Biography Resource Center, historical books and genealogy aids.

Arkansas State Library
One Capitol Mall
Little Rock, AR 72201
Tel: (501) 682-2053

Arkansas State Library: http://www.asl.lib.ar.us/

Arkansas Land Patents - pre-1908 Arkansas Land Records documenting the transfer of land ownership from the government to individuals. This data can assist family historians is placing an ancestor in a specific location and date.

Arkansas Land Patents:
http://www.worldvitalrecords.com/indexinfo.aspx?ix=blmar&kbid=1067

Arkansas Genealogical and Historical Societies

Genealogical and historical societies have access to extensive catalogues of genealogical data. They are also able to offer expert guidance for genealogical researchers. Many members are professional genealogists who are most willing to share their expertise in finding ancestors.

Arkansas Genealogical Society – journals, family histories, and ancestry charts.

Arkansas Genealogical Society
P.O. Box 26374
Little Rock, AR 72221-6374

Arkansas Genealogical Society: http://www.agsgenealogy.org/

Grand Prairie Genealogical Society – various resources

Grand Prairie Genealogical Society
c/o Stuttgart Public Library
2002 So. Buerkle St.
Stuttgart, AR 72160

Grand Prairie Genealogical Society:
http://www.rootsweb.ancestry.com/~ararkans/grandpra.htm?cj=1&netid=cj&o_xid=0001231185&o_lid=0001231185&o_sch=Affiliate+External

Northwest Arkansas Genealogical Society – probate records, deeds, military records, cemetery and burial records

Northwest Arkansas Genealogical Society
405 S. Main St
Bentonville, AR 72712
Email: genealogy@bentonvillear.com

Northwest Arkansas Genealogical Society:
http://www.rootsweb.ancestry.com/~arnwags/?cj=1&netid=cj&o_xi
d=0001231185&o_lid=0001231185&o_sch=Affiliate+External

Arkansas Historical Association – various resources

Arkansas Historical Association
416 Old Main, University of Arkansas
Fayetteville, AR 72701
Tel: 479-575-5884
Fax: 479-575-2775
Email:dludlow@uark.ed

Arkansas Historical Association:
http://arkansashistoricalassociation.org/

Central Arkansas Genealogical & Historical Society – various resources

CAGHS
PO Box 1441
North Little Rock, AR 72115

Central Arkansas Genealogical & Historical Society:
http://caghs.net/

Arkansas Family History Centers

The Family History Centers run by the LDS Church offer free access to billions of genealogical records for free to the general public. They also provide classes on genealogy and one-on-one assistance to inexperienced family historians. Here you will find a **Complete Listing of Arkansas Family History Centers**.

Complete Listing of Arkansas Family History Centers :
https://familysearch.org/locations/centerlocator

Arkansas Mailing Lists

Mailing lists are internet based facilities that use email to distribute a single message to all who subscribe to it. When information on a particular surname, new records, or any other important genealogy information related to the mailing list topic becomes available, the subscribers are alerted to it. Joining a mailing list is an excellent way to stay up to date on Arkansas genealogy research topics. Rootsweb have an extensive listing of **Arkansas Mailing Lists** on a variety of topics.

Arkansas Mailing Lists:
http://lists.rootsweb.ancestry.com/index/usa/AR/misc.html

Arkansas Message Boards

A message board is another internet based facility where people can post questions about a specific genealogy topic and have it answered by other genealogists. If you have questions about a surname, record type, or research topic, you can post your question and other researchers and genealogists will help you with the answer. You must make sure to check back regularly, as the answers are not emailed to you. The Arkansas message boards at **Rootsweb** are completely free to use.

Rootsweb:
http://boards.rootsweb.com/localities.northam.usa.states/mb.ashx

Arkansas Newspapers and Periodicals

Many genealogy periodicals and historical newspapers contain reprinted copies of family genealogies, transcripts of family Bible records, information about local records and archives, census indexes, church records, queries, land records, obituaries, court records, cemetery records, and wills. The following sites have historical Arkansas newspapers and periodicals that you can search online or on-site.

NewspaperArchive.com – largest online database of historical newspapers in the world.

NewspaperArchive.com: http://newspaperarchive.com/

University of Arkansas Library – large catalogue of historical Arkansas newspapers on microfilm.
University of Arkansas Libraries
365 N. McIlroy Ave.
Fayetteville, AR 72701-4002

University of Arkansas Library:
http://uark.libguides.com/content.php?pid=64579&sid=477152

Fort Smith Public Library - catalogue of almost 300 Arkansas periodicals

Fort Smith Public Library
3201 Rogers Avenue
Fort Smith, AR 72903
Tel: 479-783-0229
Fax: 479-782-8571

Fort Smith Public Library:
http://www.fortsmithlibrary.org/refpapers.html

Central Arkansas Library System - hundreds of magazine and journal articles

Central Arkansas Library System:
http://www.cals.lib.ar.us/research/magazines-journals.aspx

Historical Arkansas Maps and Gazetteers

Maps are an integral part of genealogical research. They help us to locate landmarks, towns, cities, parishes, states, provinces, waterways and roads and streets. They also help us to determine when and where boundary changes might have taken place, and give us a visualization of the area we're researching in. For locating place names, a gazetteer is the best possible resource for any genealogist. Gazetteers are also sometimes called "place name dictionaries", and can help you to locate the area in which you need to conduct research. Below are links to the maps and gazetteers for research in Arkansas.

Peabody GNIS Service – Arkansas:
http://peabody.research.yale.edu/cgi-bin/Query.GNIS?ST=Arkansas&SU=1
Color Landform Atlas – Arkansas:
http://fermi.jhuapl.edu/states/ar_0.html

1985 U.S. Atlas: http://www.livgenmi.com/1895/AR/

Arkansas Hometown Locator:
http://arkansas.hometownlocator.com/

Arkansas City Directories

City directories are similar to telephone directories in that they list the residents of a particular area. The difference though is what is important to genealogists, and that is they pre-date telephone directories. You can find an ancestor's information such as their street address, place of employment, occupation, or the name of their spouse. A one-stop-shop for finding city directories in Arkansas is the **Arkansas Online Historical Directories** which contains a listing of every available city and historical directory related to Arkansas.

Arkansas Online Historical Directories:
https://sites.google.com/site/onlinedirectorysite/Home/usa/ar

Arkansas Genealogical Records

Birth, Death, Marriage and Divorce Records – Birth, death, and marriage records are the most basic, yet most important records attached to your ancestor. They are generally referred to as vital records as they record vital life events. The reason for their importance is that they not only place your ancestor in a specific place at a definite time, but potentially connect the individual to other relatives. Below is a list of repositories where you can find Arkansas vital records

Arkansas Department of Health – birth and death records from February 1, 1914 through the present, marriage records from January 1917, divorce records from January 1923

Arkansas Department of Health
4815 West Markham Street
Little Rock, Arkansas 72205
Tel: 501-661-2336, 800-637-9314,501-661-2717

Arkansas Department of Health;
http://www.healthy.arkansas.gov/programsServices/certificatesVital Records/Pages/default.aspx

Family Search has birth, death, marriage, and divorce indexes dating from 1779-1950

Family Search:
https://familysearch.org/learn/wiki/en/Arkansas_Online_Genealogy_ Records

Early Black Marriages of Ft. Smith, Arkansas (1865-1867):
http://www.angelfire.com/ar/freedmen/mars.html

Census Reports

Census records are among the most important genealogical documents for placing your ancestor in a particular place at a specific time. Like BDM records, they can also lead you to other ancestors, particularly those who were living under the authority of the head of household.

Official Arkansas census records exist from 1830 -1940 and many images and indexes can be viewed online. Following are the best places to find Arkansas census records.

U.S National Archives – Arkansas census records on microfilm available from 1820

U.S National Archives:
http://www.archives.gov/research/census/nonpopulation/arkansas.html

FamilyLink.com - 1830-1940 census schedules

FamilyLink.com:
http://www.familylink.com/contentsearch.aspx?p=Arkansas

Access Genealogy: Arkansas census records from 1790

Access Genealogy:
http://www.accessgenealogy.com/census/arkansas-census-records.htm

African American Gateway – Gateway to a large collection of online African American records including; Slave censuses, Slave schedules, Slaves inhabitants lists

African American Gateway:
http://www.genealogycenter.info/africanamerican/results_afram.php?subject=ar

Arkansas Church Records

Church and synagogue records are a valuable resource, especially for baptisms, marriages, and burials that took place before 1900. There are a few challenges to locating and accessing church records, such as the multitude of religious denominations that exist. Once found however, they can reveal information about your ancestor that other records do not. You will need to at least have an idea of your ancestor's religious denomination, and in most cases you will have to visit a brick and mortar establishment to view them. Below are links archives that maintain church records, as well as a few databases that can be viewed online.

Before 1900 the largest religious denominations in Arkansas were the Baptist and Methodist Episcopal (now United Methodist). The **Family History Library** has many church records for Arkansas and several histories of local churches.

Family History Library:
http://familysearch.org/learn/wiki/en/Family_History_Library

Baptist

Arkansas Baptist State Convention Collection
Riley Library
Ouachita Baptist University
410 Ouachita
Arkedelphia, AR 71998
Tel: (870) 245-5000
Fax: (870) 245-5500

Website: http://absc.org/

Methodist

North Arkansas Conference Depository
Olin C. Bailey Library
Hendrix College
1600 Washington Street
Conway, AR 72032
Tel: (501) 336-9321
Fax: (501) 336-9001
EMail: arkmethodist@hendrix.edu

North Arkansas Conference Depository:
http://www.gcah.org/site/c.ghKJI0PHIoE/b.2858857/k.BF4D/Home.
htm

Roman Catholic

Diocese of Little Rock
2500 N. Tyler St.
Little Rock, AR 72207
Tel: (501) 664-0340

Diocese of Little Rock:
http://www.dolr.org/offices/chancery/sacramentalrecordinformation.
php

University of Arkansas - Bethlehem Church Records

University of Arkansas:
http://libinfo.uark.edu/specialcollections/findingaids/bethlehem.html
#CONTENTS OF THE

Mount Olive Baptist Church – Arkansas church records, historical
documents and
family genealogies

Mount Olive Baptist Church: http://www.shell-
family.net/history/mtolive/index_master.htm

Arkansas Military Records

More than 40 million Americans have participated in some time of war service since America was colonized. The chance of finding your ancestor amongst those records is exceptionally high. Military records can even reveal individuals who never actually served, such as those who registered for the two World Wars but were never called to duty.

Below are a number of links to websites and archives that contain Arkansas military records.

U.S. National Archives – WWI Draft registration cards, casualties lists, WWI and WWII service records, Korean War records, Vietnam War records, Civil War and Spanish-American War records, and casualties lists.

U.S. National Archives:
http://www.archives.gov/research/military/veterans/online.html

US Department of Veterans Affairs Nationwide Gravesite Locator – includes information on veterans and their family members buried in veterans and military cemeteries having a government grave marker.

US Department of Veterans Affairs Nationwide Gravesite Locator: http://gravelocator.cem.va.gov/

United States Index to Indian Wars Pension Files, 1892-1926 – military pension records of soldiers who fought in the Indian Wars between 1817 and 1898

United States Index to Indian Wars Pension Files, 1892-1926: https://familysearch.org/search/collection/1979427

Arkansas History Commission – Confederate pension records and World War 1 discharge records

Arkansas History Commission: http://www.ark-ives.com/documenting/military-records/default.aspx

Civil War Soldiers Service Records - Service records for both Union and Confederate soldiers indexed by soldier's name, rank, and unit.

Civil War Soldier Service Records:
http://go.fold3.com/civilwar_records/

Arkansas Civil War Service Records of Confederate Soldiers, 1861-1865 – service records of men who served in Confederate army in Arkansas

Arkansas Civil War Service Records of Confederate Soldiers, 1861-1865: https://familysearch.org/search/collection/1932365

Civil War Soldiers of Arkansas - database containing millions of records of soldiers who fought in the Civil War

Civil War Soldiers of Arkansas: http://civil-war-soldiers.findthedata.org/d/b/Arkansas

Arkansas Cemetery Records

As convenient as it is to search cemetery records online, keep in mind that there are a few disadvantages over visiting a cemetery in person. They are:

- Tombstone information is not always accurately transcribed
- The arrangement of the graves in a cemetery can be crucial as family members are often buried next to each other or in the same grave. This arrangement is not always preserved in the alphabetical indexes that are found online.

With that information in mind, the following websites have databases that can be searched online for Arkansas Cemetery records.

Arkansas Gravestones Project – almost one million gravestone photos from around the state

Arkansas Gravestones Project: http://arkansasgravestones.org/

African American Cemeteries Online – African American, slave, and Native American cemetery records

African American Cemeteries Online: http://africanamericancemeteries.com/ar/

Access Genealogy – huge database of Arkansas cemetery record transcriptions

Access Genealogy: http://www.accessgenealogy.com/cemetery/arkansas.htm

Find a Grave – over 100 million grave records can be searched on this site. Search can be conducted by name, location, or cemetery name.

Find a Grave : http://www.findagrave.com/

Interment.net - A free online database containing approximately 4 million cemetery records from around the world.

Interment.net: http://www.interment.net/

Arkansas Tombstone Transcription Project - death and burial records

Arkansas Tombstone Transcription Project: http://www.usgwtombstones.org/arkansas/arkansas.html

Billion Graves – as the name implies, you can search a billion records including headstone photos, transcriptions, cemetery records, and grave locations.

Billion Graves: http://billiongraves.com/pages/search/index.php#cemetery

Arkansas Obituaries

Obituaries can reveal a wealth about our ancestor and other relatives. You can search our **Arkansas Newspaper Obituaries Listings** from hundreds of Arkansas newspapers online for free.

Arkansas Newspaper Obituaries Listings: http://obituarieshelp.org/arkansas_newspaper_obituaries.html

Arkansas Wills and Probate Records

Probate records of Arkansas have been kept by the probate or county courts which can be located via an **Online Directory**. The documents found in a probate packet may include a complete inventory of a person's estate, newspaper entries, witness testimony, a copy of a will, list of debtors and creditors, names of executors or trustees, names of heirs. They can not only tell you about the ancestor you're currently researching, but lead to other ancestors. Most of these records must be accessed at a county court or clerk's office, but some can be found online as well. The **Family History Library** has microfilm copies of many Arkansas probate records.

Online Directory: https://courts.arkansas.gov/directories/county-courts

Family History Library:
http://familysearch.org/learn/wiki/en/Family_History_Library

Arkansas History Commission – records from each of Arkansas's seventy-five counties including county court records, wills, deeds, probate court records, and tax records

Arkansas History Commission : http://www.ark-ives.com/documenting/county_records.aspx

Arkansas Immigration and Naturalization Records

The naturalization process generated many types of records, including petitions, declarations of intention, and oaths of allegiance. These records can provide family historians with information such as a person's birth date and place of birth, immigration year, marital status, spouse information, occupation, witnesses' names and addresses, and more.

Naturalization records were generally filed in the circuit courts in each Arkansas County. Many of the counties have pre-1907 records. Some naturalization papers have been filed in the U.S. District Courts located in Little Rock, Fort Smith, and Fort Worth, Texas.

The National Archives-Southwest Region (Fort Worth) has an index of naturalization records for the years 1809-1906.

The National Archives-Southwest Region (Fort Worth): http://www.archives.gov/fort-worth/

There was little settlement by Europeans during the time of French and Spanish rule, 1686 to 1803. The Louisiana Territory Census of 1810 listed only 1,062 non-Native American residents in the entire District of Arkansas.

The Cotton Boom in 1818 led to an earnest increase in immigration and many Scottish, Irish, and English moved to the are, often bringing slaves with them. Later families from Poland settled in Pulaski, and Italians flocked to the north-west area of the state.

Records of the **Bureau of Indian Affairs** have been transcribed in Jack D. Baker, Cherokee Emigration Rolls, 1817-1835, while the **National Archives** has passenger from 1878-1960. The **United States Index to Passenger Arrivals, Atlantic and Gulf Ports, 1820-1874** can be searched online. The **Native American Rolls** at Access Genealogy are an excellent source for tracking Native Americans who were displaced from their homelands.

Bureau of Indian Affairs: http://www.bia.gov/

National Archives:
http://www.nationalarchives.gov.uk/records/looking-for-person/passengers.htm

United States Index to Passenger Arrivals, Atlantic and Gulf Ports, 1820-1874:
https://familysearch.org/search/collection/1921756

Native American Rolls:
http://www.accessgenealogy.com/native/rolls.htm

Native American Records

The **National Archives** - information about American Indians who maintained their ties to Federally-recognized Tribes (1830-1970).

National Archives: http://www.archives.gov/research/native-americans/

Bureau of Indian Affairs

Bureau of Indian Affairs: http://www.bia.gov/

Missing Matriarchs – Resources for Researching Female Arkansas Ancestors

Looking for female ancestors requires an adjustment of how we view traditional records sources. A woman's identity was often under that of her husband, and often individual records for them can be difficult to locate. The following resources are effective in locating female ancestors in Arkansas where traditional records may not reveal them.

Marriage and Divorce Records

Marriage records have been recorded in the county clerk's office since 1820. State registration commenced in 1917 and can be found at the **Division of Vital Records** in Little Rock. The **Arkansas Historical Commission** has selected county records of divorces from 1797-1950 on microfilm. Other county records have been filmed as such:

- Benton County Clerk marriage records 1861-1952, (film 1034660 ff.), Benton County Circuit Court records 1837-1884 (film 1035157 ff.), and Benton County Chancery Court records, 1843-1952 (film 1995053 ff.) at the Benton County Courthouse in Bentonville.
- Pulaski County Clerk marriage records 1838-1851 (index) and 1820-1971 (film 1302792 ff.), Pulaski County Chancery Court divorce records, 1882-1900 (film 1302850 ff.) at the Pulaski Courthouse in Little Rock.

Division of Vital Records:
http://www.cdc.gov/nchs/w2w/arkansas.htm

Arkansas History Commission link to: http://www.ark-ives.com/documenting/county_records.aspx

Bibliographies

1. *Arkansas Colonials: A Collection of French and Spanish Records Listing Early Europeans in the Arkansas, 1686-1804,* Morris, S. Arnold (Grand Prairie Historical Society, 1986)
2. *Confederate Women of Arkansas in the Civil War* Michael B. Dougan (M&M Press 1993)
3. *Behold: Our Work was Good: A Handbook of Arkansas Women's History* Elizabeth Jacoway, (Women's History Institute, 1987)
4. *The Seed of Sally Good'n: A Black Family in Arkansas, 1833-1953* Ruth Polk Patterson (University of Kentucky Press, 1983)

Selected Resources for Arkansas Women's History

Arkansas State University Museum
Arkansas State University
PO Box 490
State University, AR 72467

Arkansas Women's History Institute
PO Box 77
Little Rock, AR 72217

Women's Studies Program
University of Arkansas at Little Rock
2801 South University
Little Rock, AR 72204

Common Arkansas Surnames

The following surnames are among the most common in Arkansas. The list is by no means exhaustive. If your surname doesn't appear in the list it doesn't mean that you have no Arkansas connections, only that your surname may be less common.

Adams, Aldridge, Avant, Bates, Baxter, Campbell, Carter, Chapman, Gogburn, Cotton, Cunningham, Dobbs, Ellington, Farmer, Fields, Freeman, Fry, Garret, Golden, Goodman, Hardy, Hartman, Hathcock, Henson, House, Jackson, Johnson, Jones, Kelly, Kirby, Lamb, Larson, McConnell, McCullar, McDonald, Menasco, Manasco, Miller, Nelson, O'Neil, Pettit, Philips, Prowse, Qualls, Rice, Roberts, Rowland, Scott, Sharpe, Simpson, Smalling, Speer, Stewart, Tackett, Thompson, Walker, Wallace, Whiesenhunt, Whitehouse, Yarbrough

About the Author

Gary L. Morris worked from 2009 to 2014 as a professional researcher for a major player in the genealogy field. After tracing his family lineage back to 1683, he found that genealogy could be an expensive undertaking. As such, has decided to publish these helpful guides to share the valuable free information he has discovered during his career to help others trace their family lineages as inexpensively as possible. An avid genealogist himself, he hopes you will find this guide factual, thorough, helpful, and most of all, effective in helping you to find your family members.

Notes